by SHAKTA KAUR KHALSA

Fly Like

YOGA FOR CHILDREN

A Butterfly

Sterling Publishing Co., Inc.
New York

APPROVED BY THE KUNDALINI RESEARCH INSTITUTE

Library of Congress Cataloging-in-Publication Data

Khalsa, Shakta Kaur, 1950–
    Fly like a butterfly: yoga for children/Shakta Kaur Khalsa.
    p.   cm.
    Summary: Introduces the philosophy and poses of yoga
with the help of photographs, stoires, and movement games.
    ISBN 0-915801-84-1
    1. Yoga, Hatha, for children—Juvenile literature. 2. Exercise for children—
Juvenile literature. [1. Yoga.] I. Title.
    RA781.7.K48   1998
    613.7'046'083—dc21

98-24999
CIP
AC

10 9 8 7

Published by Sterling Publishing Co., Inc.
387 Park Avenue South, New York, NY 10016
© 1998 by Shakta Kaur Khalsa
Distributed in Canada by Sterling Publishing
C/o Canadian Manda Group, 165 Dufferin Street
Toronto, Ontario, Canada M6K 3H6
Distributed in Great Britain and Europe by Chris Lloyd at Orca Book Services
Stanley House, Fleets Lane, Poole, BH15 3AJ England
Distributed in Australia by Capricorn Link (Australia) Pty. Ltd.
P.O. Box 704, Windsor, NSW 2756 Australia

Sterling ISBN 13: 978-0-915801-84-8
    ISBN 10: 0-915801-84-1

For information about custom editions, special sales, premium and
corporate purchases, please contact Sterling Special Sales
Department at 800-805-5489 or specialsales@sterlingpub.com

table of contents

DEDICATED TO ALL CHILDREN,

EVERYWHERE

acknowledgments

THIS BOOK COMES
BY THE GRACE
OF THE ONE.

THANKS AND ACKNOWLEDGMENTS GO TO:

Yogi Bhajan, as the giver of this wonderful yoga, and
countless other blessings. Thank you, sir!

My husband, Kartar Singh, for vision and steadiness. Thanks for your love
and unfailing willingness to shoulder responsibility.

My son, Ram Das Singh, for his very genuine love and enthusiasm.

Guru Atma Kaur Khalsa, for her expertise, humor, and kindness.

Jan Carson, for her beautiful photos and gentle, easy manner.

Thanks to Amrit Kaur Khalsa for her fine illustrations.

Thanks to the parents of the children in the book
for their enthusiastic support.

Rachel Gaffney, my editor, who is an answer to my prayer for this book.

Dedication, know-how, and fine attunement—all in one publisher!

Jody Grossman for her innate ability to appreciate and inspire.

My mother and father, Grace and Howard Meyers, whose loving
kindness have helped this project more than they know.

The Boyd School and Mary Ann Woosley for their cooperation.

Giles Gouldsmith, for crucial computer help.

Susan Bagette, for guidance in starting this project.

Adarsh Kaur Khalsa, for sisterly support.

Sat Kirpal Kaur Khalsa and everyone at KRI
for their helpful suggestions.

A VERY HEARTFELT THANKS TO ALL
THE CHILDREN IN THE PHOTOS:

Sarah Beckworth, Torie Lyons, Erica Harkins, Leslie Harkins,
Shanthi Wickramasinghe, Nicole Yu, Kelsy Alston, Hailey Edgemond,
Andrew Jones, Ella Jones, Ram Das Singh Khalsa,
Sat Mandir Singh Khalsa, Guru Amrit Kaur Khalsa, Hari Akal Singh Khalsa,
Simone Grossman, Hamish Isaac, Zachary Isaac, Madeleine Foster,
Rachel Adam, Cory Sterling, Tara Ice-Wright, and Byron Bizzle.

YOUR BOUNDLESS SPIRIT RISES
TO GREET THE READER!

for parents and teachers

greetings and congratulations on joining the ever-growing group of parents and teachers who are aware of the benefits of yoga for children. Although yoga has enjoyed popularity with adults for many years, it is only recently that we have come to understand how helpful it can be for children in their formative years, increasing their self-awareness, building their self-esteem, and strengthening their bodies—truly a welcomed oasis in a culture that offers little in the way of mindful yet active play.

The yoga in this book is dynamic, bursting with imaginary animals and stories which capture the children, who in their delight have no clue how healthy and relaxed they are becoming. One could almost call it "creative movement," except that it contains all the essential ingredients of yoga—breath awareness, mind-body fitness, and the opportunity to experience the "self within."

The body is made to do yoga. Yoga postures and angles create certain pressures to stimulate the body and brain, making the necessary changes to become a healthy, happy, and whole person.

INSTRUCTIONAL TIPS

- If the child is too young to read for herself, read the instructions to her slowly and with expression. She may need you to be involved in order to keep focused and follow the exercise sets in sequence.

- Encourage children to inhale and exhale through the nose unless specified.

- Follow each exercise with a deep breath or two.

- Allow for a short relaxation (15 seconds or so) on the floor after more strenuous exercises.

- Use a soft rug or mat on the floor and a light shawl or blanket for covering during relaxation or meditation.

- Encourage children to close their eyes once they understand how to do the exercise so they can feel it.

- Vary the structure. Some of the sets, for example "Crazy, Mixed-Up Yoga," do not need to be followed in any particular order. Others, such as "The Yoga Mountain Story," make sense only if followed in order.

- Monitor time. How long does it take to do each exercise? Generally 20 seconds to 1 minute is good for children under 6, 1 minute to 1-1/2 minutes for children 6 and older. Some children will enjoy using a timer to keep track of the time of each exercise. For example, a yoga class I teach with 3- to 6-year-old children will last for 15 minutes and a class of 7- to 9-year-olds will extend to 25 minutes.

- Know that the photographs in the book are not always precise renderings of the pose. Pay attention to the written instructions and give these priority over the photographs when you are unsure how to proceed.

- Let your creativity shine as you find ways to engage the child in the practice of yoga. Count to 25, see if he can go longer than the last time, have her "lead" you in an exercise. These are some ways to keep the focus and provide a positive experience. During meditation, put a little treat beside her, or under her mat, to let her know that meditation is sweet. The children in my classes love hugging the little animal puppet who comes to wake them up after relaxation. You will discover your own special rituals for yoga. And please remember to allow the experience to take its own form—don't be too concerned about following a fixed routine. It is more important that the child have a positive experience, than a "perfect" one!

Most of all, enjoy the health, happiness, and blessings that come from doing yoga. Good luck to you and your children!

welcome to your very own yoga book!

Please read this page first or have an adult read it to you.

Yoga makes you feel good. You may like to do yoga whenever you feel like it. You may like to do it every day at a certain time, like when you wake up in the morning, or before bed. It is up to you!

Do you know you have a teacher inside? Well, you do! And how do you find your inner teacher? You "tune in" to yourself from the inside. Every time you want to do yoga, sit down in a quiet place. Then look at Chapter 1, called TUNE IN TO BEGIN. Start there.

Choose the yoga that you want to do. Most of the time you are doing yoga you will be breathing through your nose. By making the breath strong and being aware of it coming in and out, you relax and become fearless. In math it looks like this: strong breath + attention on your breath = NO FEAR!

Be adventurous! Try keeping your eyes closed during the exercises. Look inside instead of outside, and see what you find.

After yoga take a rest—the yoga will keep working on you while you rest. Relax completely, like you are going to sleep. You may want to cover yourself with your favorite light blanket. When you are done, do the wake-up exercises. If you would like to do a meditation, this is a good time, because after yoga your body and mind are ready to be still.

People have been using yoga for thousands of years to be healthy, to feel happy, and to know who they are. You might say "I know who I am, I am Sarah!" or "I am Michael." But there is more to you than you think! Yoga can help you experience your self, your whole self. And the best part is—it's a lot of fun! So let's get started!

FIGURE 1-A

1. tune in to begin

Sit with your legs crossed and your back straight. Bring your hands together at your heart. Press the palms of your hands together, and press them into the center of your chest. Close your eyes. Feel as though you can see out from the center of your forehead, close to where your eyes meet. At the same time, feel a warm glow in your heart. Now breathe in and out slowly and deeply through your nose. Do this three times. Figure 1-A

now I am going to share with you the way my teacher taught me to tune in. It is done by creating a contact sound. This sound contacts your inner teacher, and connects you to all yoga teachers, sort of like the beautiful blue ocean connects one wave to another! When you tune in this way, you are saying, "I am making a special space so the best can come to me!" Here's how you do it:

Sit and focus the same way you did while reading the first paragraph. Now, on each of the three deep breaths, repeat the following sounds as you breathe out:

Ong   Na–mo   Gu–ru Dev   Na–mo

It means, "I greet the wise teacher within me and outside of me."

Make your voice clear and strong, and feel it come from your heart.

FIGURE 2-A

2. let's warm up!

RIDE YOUR BUMPY CAMEL: Begin by sitting with your legs crossed. Take hold of your outside ankle. This is your saddle. We are going to ride our camel across the desert. Breathe in deeply as you stretch your body forward, chest and stomach out. Breathe out as you slump back, spine is curved, chest is caved in. Keep moving this way faster and faster. Remember, it is very hot in the desert, and we want to get across it quickly! Figures 2-A and 2-B

FIGURE 2-B

FIGURE 2-C

COBRA SNAKE: When we got across the desert what did we see but a BIG COBRA SNAKE! Lie down on your stomach. Put your hands under your shoulders, and push up until your arms are straight. Curve your chest upward and look up at the ceiling. Stretch out of your shoulders. Relax your back and stretch up as far as you can while keeping your stomach and legs on the ground. Look up and begin breathing in deeply from the nose. Now begin HISSING as you breathe out through the mouth. Be a fierce Cobra Snake! Keep going for a minute or two. Then inhale and stretch your tail up (your legs). Try to touch your head and "tail" together. Can you do it? Now come down slowly, bending the arms. Relax on the floor with your head turned to one side, arms by your side, and breathe for a minute. Figures 2-C and 2-D

FIGURE 2-D

7

BICYCLE: Roll over onto your back, lift your legs up in the air, and begin bicycling away from that Cobra Snake! Move in large, fast circles until we get home. Now stretch your legs up straight. Take hold of your feet or ankles, whichever you can reach with your legs straight. Inhale and stretch. Release your legs, rock forward on an exhale, and sit up. We made it home! Figures 2-E and 2-F

FIGURE 2-E

FIGURE 2-F

FIGURE 2-G

WASHING MACHINE: Our clothes have gotten dirty from all our traveling, so let's wash them! Sit with your legs crossed. Stretch your arms up and put your hands on your shoulders, fingers in front and thumbs in back. Point your elbows out to the side, and begin twisting side to side. Breathe in as you twist to one side. Breathe out as you twist to the other side. Make a swishing sound as you exhale, and wash those clothes! Figure 2-G

FIGURE 2-H

DRYER: Are your clothes clean? Then let's dry them! Bring your arms in front of your chest, and begin circling your hands around each other. How fast can you go without your hands touching each other? Look at your hands and breathe deeply as you move faster. Figure 2-H

FIGURE 2-1

BUTTERFLY: Now bring the soles of your feet together and hold onto your feet with both hands. Your feet are as close to your body as is comfortable. Begin flapping your legs. These are your butterfly wings. Let's sing the butterfly song.

Repeat the song a few times and keep flapping your legs. After you finish the song, inhale, breathing in deeply. Exhale, breathe out, and bring your head down to your feet. Shhh! Our butterfly is going to sleep. Figures 2-1 and 2-J

butterfly song

C   Dm
FLY LIKE A BUTTERFLY   FLY LIKE A BUTTER-FLY

C   G
FLY LIKE A BUTTER-FLY   IN THE SKY!

C   Dm
FLY LIKE A BUTTER-FLY   FLY LIKE A BUTTER-FLY

C   G   C
FLY LIKE A BUTTER-FLY   IN THE SKY.

FIGURE 2-J

FIGURE 3-A

3. the yoga mountain story

"Once there was a tall, beautiful mountain." Begin on your hands and knees and lift your bottom up into the air to move into mountain pose, also called triangle pose. The feet are flat on the ground, hip distance apart. The hands are spread shoulder-width apart on the ground, supporting your body. Breathe long and deep. Relax your head down and keep stretching. Figure 3-A

FIGURE 3-B

"This mountain had tall, tall trees on it." Come into tree pose. Stand on one leg with the other leg bent so it folds into the straight leg. If you're standing on your right leg, your left foot can be placed inside your right thigh. Your left leg will form a triangle. Balance with your palms together at the heart. Choose a spot across the room from you and keep your steady focus there. This will help you balance. When you feel very steady, slowly bring your arms up straight over your head with your palms still together. Breathe gently and stretch up tall. Now switch legs and be a tall tree on the other side of the mountain! Figure 3-B

"Now on this mountain there lived a very beautiful bird." Sit on your heels, keeping your back straight. Bring your arms straight out to the sides and let your fingers touch the floor. Keep your arms and hands straight and pull your arms up over your head, touching the backs of your hands together. Breathe in as you pull your "wings" up, then breathe out as you bring your "wings" back down. Keep going for a minute or two. Go fast and powerfully. Figures 3-C and 3-D

FIGURE 3-C

FIGURE 3-D

14

FIGURE 3-E

"Down in the valley, there was a town. The town had many people in it. The people heard that there was gold up on the mountain, and they wanted it for themselves. So they began running up the mountain as fast as they could." Begin jogging in place. Lift your knees up high and alternately push and pull your arms back and forth as you run up the mountain. Don't forget to breathe! Figure 3-E

FIGURE 3-F

"Once they got to the mountain, they picked up their axes and began chopping the mountain to get the gold inside." Stand up with your feet apart. Interlace your fingers and clasp your hands together out front. Breathe in and stretch your arms up and back while leaning back as far as you can. Then breathe out and chop that mountain, bringing your arms down toward the ground. Keep up the powerful strokes. Figure 3-F

FIGURE 3-G

"The mountain became smaller and smaller as they chopped it." Come into the mountain pose again, but this time begin walking the feet up toward your hands. Keep your legs as straight as you can while walking in very tiny steps. When your feet reach your hands, step your legs back into mountain pose again. Keep walking up and stepping back for a minute or two. Figure 3-G

FIGURE 3-H

"The beautiful bird was sad when she saw what was happening to the mountain. She had an idea that could help the mountain. She began flying high in the sky, faster and faster, higher and higher, searching for a special cloud to help her." Sit on your heels again. Bring your arms straight out to each side, touch your fingertips to the ground, and begin flying with your "wings." Let the backs of your hands touch above your head. Inhale up and exhale down. Go high and find that special cloud! Figure 3-H

FIGURE 3-I

"She found the cloud—a big, gray rain cloud. The rain cloud was happy to help the mountain. It puffed itself up until it was as big as the mountain." Sit on your heels. Reach back and take hold of your heels. Kneel up as you push your stomach forward. Puff your chest out and put your head back. This is called Camel Pose. We will call it Rain Cloud in this story. If you cannot hold your heels while doing this pose, you can try supporting yourself with your hands on the floor behind you instead. Stay breathing deeply for a minute. Come out of the posture slowly, fold your body forward, and put your forehead on the floor for a few seconds. Figures 3-I and 3-J

FIGURE 3-J

FIGURE 3-K

"The rain cloud began to blow a great wind. The wind got stronger and stronger." Stand up with your feet wide apart. Put your hands on your hips, bend over, and make a circle with your upper body. When you circle to the right side, breathe in. As you circle to the left side, breathe out in a "cannon breath." This means to shoot the breath out through the mouth powerfully and rapidly. After several circles to one side, make your circle go the other way. Now you will breathe in on the left side, and out on the right with the cannon breath. Figure 3-K

FIGURE 3-L

"Thunder began to roar, and lightning began crashing down onto the mountain." Still standing, bring the feet closer together. Inhale and stretch back with the arms overhead. Exhale and stretch the arms down to the ground, keeping your knees slightly bent, and again using the cannon breath. This is the lightning. Be strong and powerful! Keep going for a minute. Figure 3-L

FIGURE 3-M

"The storm crashed on the mountain. Huge boulders were torn from the mountain and came rolling and tumbling down." Lie on your back. Tuck your legs into your chest, put your head between your knees, and wrap your arms around your legs. Rock back and forth on your spine. Roll all the way up to a sitting position, then rock all the way back to your neck. Roll back and forth several times. Figure 3-M

FIGURE 3-N

"When the huge rocks began falling on the people, they began running home crying, 'Let's get out of here! Let's go home!'" Stand up and begin running in place. Go as fast as you can. Alternately push and pull your arms straight out in front and lift your knees high. Use a strong breath. Push and pull your breath too! Figure 3-N

FIGURE 3-O

"When they got home they said, 'We will never bother that mountain again! It is too dangerous!' So now the mountain is once again strong and tall, and it is the home to many animals, including the beautiful bird."

Come back into mountain pose. Breathe long and deep and keep your arms and legs straight. Figure 3-O

THE END

4. an animal adventure

Let's go on a little adventure. First we will jog through the jungle. Stand up and begin jogging. Lift your knees high and breathe deeply. We are jogging through the thick green jungle. Let's keep jogging for a minute. Stop! What is that animal up high in the tree?

It's a COBRA SNAKE! Come into Cobra pose. Lie on your stomach. Put your hands on the floor under your shoulders. Stretch your upper body up high, with your arms straight and your stomach resting on the ground. Stretch your head as far back as you can and HISS! You are a very fierce cobra snake! Keep stretching and hissing on the exhale for a minute.

FIGURE 4-A

Then breathe in and lift your bottom up. Breathe out and curl back onto your heels with your forehead on the floor, legs tucked underneath. Your arms are stretched out straight in front of you. Now breathe in and stretch back up into Cobra pose, breathe out and curl up. Keep stretching out and curling up for a minute. Figures 4-A and 4-B

FIGURE 4-B

next in the jungle we see an ELEPHANT. Stand up. Bend forward with your arms hanging down. Clasp your hands together with your fingers interlocked. Now walk around the room, bent over, and swinging your trunk. After a minute, stretch your trunk high up into the air, lean back and let out a big elephant sound like a horn! Figures 4-C and 4-D

FIGURE 4-C

FIGURE 4-D

FIGURE 4-E

In this part of the jungle, there are playful MONKEYS. Begin doing Monkey Jumps. Here's how: Bend over with your hands touching the floor and your feet spread a little apart. Keep your legs pretty straight; bend them only a little to jump. Now inhale and jump up so that your hands and feet leave the ground at the same time. Then exhale and come down so that your hands and feet touch the ground at almost the same time. Your tail stays up in the air when you land. Go fast and jump in place. Can you do 10, 20—how about 30? Figure 4-E

FIGURE 4-F

hat animal do we see next in our jungle adventure? A big, furry LION! Sit down on your heels. Put your hands on the floor in front of you. Lean forward on your hands, and squeeze your shoulders up toward your ears. Keep your eyes open, looking straight ahead. Open your mouth and stick out your tongue as far as you can. Begin a soft purring sound in your throat as you breathe in and out through your mouth. KEEP UP! Remember to keep squeezing the shoulders up. You should feel very strong. Figure 4-F

FIGURE 4-G

We have come to some tall, tall grass. We will have to climb through it. Stand up. Lift your left leg and right arm high up in the air. Stretch! Now lift your right leg and left arm high up and stretch. Keep going through the tall, tall grass. Figure 4-G

FIGURE 4-H

now we have reached the other side, and we find ourselves at the ocean! Look way out in the water. It's a SEAL! Lie down on your stomach and bring your arms out in front with the palms of your hands flat together. Stretch your body up into Seal Pose. Pull your legs up without bending them. Pull your arms up too. To arch your back you will have to use both your back and leg muscles. Now clap your hands and bark like a seal. Do this for a minute, then begin swimming, rocking side to side. Keep going! Figure 4-H

FIGURE 4-1

Look at the sandy beach. Do you see any little creatures here? Hey, there's a
CRAB! Come into Crab Pose by sitting on the floor with your legs bent and close
to your body. Put your hands in back of you on the floor. Lean back and lift your
body up off the ground. Begin walking sideways with your hands and feet, keeping
your body off the ground the whole time. Go one direction, then the other.
Figure 4-1

FIGURE 4-J

Our farm is just over some big hills, so now we must go over those hills. Stretch your legs out straight in front of you. Reach down with your hands on your legs. Breathe in as you stretch up straight, breathe out as you stretch down to your legs. Let your hands slide down your legs to your toes as you go forward, and come back up as you sit up straight—up the hill and down the hill, up the hill and down the hill. Figure 4-J

ere we are at the pond by our farm. Look in the water–do you see the FROGS? They are exercising on their lily pads. Let's join them. Squat down with your heels close together and slightly off the ground. Put your fingertips on the floor in front of your feet. Inhale and straighten your legs, bringing your head close to your knees. Keep your fingers on the floor.

Exhale and squat down again. Do 10 or 15 "froggies." Are you warmed up now? Figures 4-K and 4-L

FIGURE 4-K

FIGURE 4-L

FIGURE 4-M

hen let's start hopping all around the pond. Leap up high and land sitting straight up in your squatting position. Ribbit! Figure 4-M

et's see what is happening on the farm. There are two of our animal friends in the barnyard—a CAT and a COW. Come onto your hands and knees. Keep your back straight. Breathe in. Stretch your head back as your back curves. Moo! It's Mrs. Cow! Now breathe out and stretch your head down so your chin is tucked into your chest. Let your back arch up. Meow! It's Mr. Cat! Keep stretching and arching back and forth in Cat and Cow. Pose for a minute or two. Then breathe in and stretch back one last time into Cow. Let's hear a big mooooo! Figures 4-N and 4-O

FIGURE 4-N

FIGURE 4-O

FIGURE 4-P

et's go into the barn now and what do we see? Our DONKEY is
doing Donkey Kicks! Keep your hands on the ground with your feet
on the floor. Now begin kicking your legs up high in the air using
your hands on the ground for balance. Hee Haw! Hee Haw! Keep
kicking for a minute. Figure 4-P

FIGURE 4-Q

now we have reached our home. Let's go to our cozy bedroom and lie down on the bed. It feels so good to relax after our big Animal Adventure, doesn't it? Lie down on your back with your legs and arms straight and relaxed. Just breathe and relax with your eyes closed for a few minutes. Relax,   Figure 4-Q

relax,

relax....

FIGURE 5-A

5. what—more animals?!!

Use some of these to replace animals in AN ANIMAL ADVENTURE or...make up your own animal story!!

SPIDER STRETCH: Stand up with your feet spread apart slightly. Squat down with your feet flat on the floor. Reach through your legs with your arms and put your hands flat on the floor behind you. Breathe and bounce your tail up and down a little to stretch more. Is your spider stretched out enough yet? Figure 5-A

FIGURE 5-B

BEAR WALK: Stand up with your hands and feet on the ground. Begin walking around the room using opposite hands and feet. When your left leg moves forward, your right arm moves forward. Stretch out but keep your legs and arms mostly straight. At the end, growl like a fierce bear! Figure 5-B

FIGURE 5-C

FISH POSE: Sit on or between your heels. Now gently lie back so that your back and head are flat on the ground. Let your arms be relaxed by your sides. Breathe and feel like a cozy fish in the water. Relax for a minute. Figure 5-C

FIGURE 5-D

BUZZING BEE: Sitting on your heels, stretch your arms out to the sides with your hands and fingers straight out. Begin very quick flaps with the arms perfectly straight. You will only move a few inches up and down. Go fast like the wings of a buzzing bee. They move so fast that you can't even see them! Try it. Buzz! Buzz! Figure 5-D

FIGURE 5-E

BUTTERFLY-COCOON: Lie down on your back. Breathe out and pull your legs up into your chest and hold them there with your arms. Now you are in your cocoon. Breathe in and bring your legs up and your arms out to the side. You are now a butterfly. Your legs will be pointing out a little in front of you, not exactly straight up. If you are doing it right, you will feel that your stomach muscles are holding your legs up. Keep going out and in slowly and gracefully with deep breaths for a minute. Feel beautiful! Figures 5-E and 5-F

FIGURE 5-F

KANGAROO HOPS: Stand up. Crouch down with your hands close together like kangaroo paws. Now inhale and spring up high, leaping up like a happy kangaroo. Keep going, making sure you crouch, then leap up. Go for a minute. Figures 5-G and 5-H

FIGURE 5-G

FIGURE 5-H

FIGURE 5-1

DINOSAUR WALK: Stand up. Now bend over and take hold of your ankles. Keep your legs straight and watch where you are going as you lumber around the room like a big, heavy dinosaur. Keep up! Figure 5-1

FIGURE 5-J

PENGUIN: From the land of snow and ice comes our friend the penguin. Sit on your heels, then kneel up. Take hold of your ankles in back of you. Walk around on your knees, holding your feet up close to your body. Watch out—you've got to keep your balance on the ice! Be sure to do this exercise on a well-padded floor or mat. Figure 5-J

FIGURE 6-A

6. crazy, mixed-up yoga

Have fun picking out your favorites! Want to try some new ones this time?

NO HANDS STAND: Stand with your arms up over your head. Cross your legs and sit down without using your hands. Get up without using your hands. Can you do it 5 times? 10 times? Great! Figure 6-A

FIGURE 6-B

BUBBLE POP: Lie down on your back. Bend your legs so that your feet are on the ground close to your bottom. Grab onto your ankles and push your body up by pressing your feet down. Make a big bubble out of your body. On "three" let your bubble pop—ready? One...two...three...pop down! Breathe in when you bubble up, out when you pop down. Keep going. Figure 6-B

FIGURE 6-C

SLIDING BOARD: Sit with your feet in front of you and your hands in back on the floor. Breathe in and push yourself up into a kind of backwards push-up. Make yourself into a perfectly straight sliding board by pushing your stomach up and pointing your toes away from you. Count to 10, 20, or 30. Can you go for 50? Figure 6-C

FIGURE 6-D

WHEEL POSE: Lie down on your back with your knees bent so that your feet are close to your tail. Bend your elbows and put your hands on the floor by your head with your fingers pointing toward your shoulders. Push up so you are on just your hands and feet. Make sure they are steady. Your body will arch like a wheel. Have a person "spot" you or help hold you up, if you need to. Breathe in this position for a minute. Then come down gently and relax on your back for a minute. Figure 6-D

FIGURE 6-E

ARCHER: Stand up with your right foot in front, pointing forward, and your left foot in back pointing slightly to the side. Lean into the front leg by bending it. As you do that, bring your arms up with your right arm straight out in front, and your left arm bent by your shoulder, as though you are pulling back on a bow. Look down your arm, lean in deeper, and breathe. Stare at your target straight ahead. You are a brave archer, feel it! Now breathe in deeply, bend your front leg deeply—hold it—and let go of your arrow. Exhale. Switch legs and do the same on the other side. Figure 6-E

FIGURE 6-F

TRAIN RIDE: Sit on your heels. Put your hands on your legs. Begin to ride the train by pushing your chest out when you breathe in, and slumping back when you breathe out. Start out slowly, and as your train gets going, start to speed up. All aboard! Figure 6-F

FIGURE 6-G

EASY "V" POSE: Sit with your legs out straight in front. Lean back with your hands on the floor behind you for support. Inhale and lift your legs up in a "V" shape. Keep breathing and hold the pose for a half-minute. Can you do a minute? Figure 6-G

FIGURE 6-H

BALANCE POSE: Sit with your legs out straight in front. Lean back as before and bring your legs up straight, keeping them together. Bring your arms out straight in front of you for balance. Concentrate on holding yourself up and breathe. Keep up as long as you can. You are GREAT! Figure 6-H

FIGURE 6-1

CANDLE: This is also called Shoulder Stand. Lie down on your back. Lift your legs and lower back high into the air. Support your back by putting your hands on your back near your waist with your elbows on the floor. Push yourself up so that you are resting on your shoulders. Be a very straight candle. Breathe in and out and keep straightening. Keep your head facing forward. If you need help, ask someone to "spot" you. Make sure when you come down that you roll out slowly. Inch your back down first, then your legs. Exhale as you come down. Figure 6-1

FIGURE 6-J

CANDLE SPLIT: Come up into Candle. When you feel steady, open your legs like you are doing a split in the air. Hold them open as you breathe, or inhale as you open them, and exhale as you close them. Continue for a minute or two, then bring your legs together and come down the same way as Candle—very carefully! Figure 6-J

FIGURE 6-K

PLOW: Plow is a lot like Candle, except that your legs go over your head behind you. Support yourself with your hands on your waist if you need to, or else you can rest your arms down. Breathe, relax into the exercise and stretch your legs back for a minute. Can your feet touch the floor behind your head? If they can, push your heels away from your body for a deeper stretch. Figure 6-K

If your feet don't reach the ground, you can use a wall to help you. Roll back into the plow near a wall. Put your feet on the wall. Stretch, breathe, and relax. You may find you can inch your feet further down the wall now! When you are ready, roll out very slowly, massaging your back against the floor.

FIGURE 6-L

WALKING IN PLOW: Be in Candle (see figure 6-1). Then bring one leg down into Plow as you breathe out. Breathe in and come back into Candle. Breathe out and bring the other leg down into Plow. Keep walking for a minute. Roll out slowly. Figure 6-L

FIGURE 6-M

TRAIN WHEELS: Sit with your legs crossed. Bring your arms to your sides with your elbows bent. Make fists of your hands. As you punch one arm out straight in front, breathe in. As you punch the other arm out, bring the first arm back to your side and breathe out powerfully through your nose. Keep switching arms and punching out. Listen to your breath— does it sound like train wheels? Figures 6-M and 6-N

FIGURE 6-N

FIGURE 6-0

SHOULDER **SHRUGS:** Did you ever feel like someone was bugging you? Well, this exercise will help you shrug it off! Sit in cross-legged position. Put your hands on your knees. Breathe in and stretch your shoulders up to your ears. Try to touch your shoulders to your ears. Then breathe out and let them drop down. Keep your head and neck still and just move your shoulders. Start out slowly and get faster and faster, but make it a big stretch each time. Shrug off all your problems—go! Figure 6-O

FIGURE 6-P

NECK ROLLS: Sit with your legs crossed. Drop your head down but keep your back straight. Breathe in as you roll your head to one side and then to the back. Do not drop your head all the way back. Breathe out as your head comes around to the other side. Go slowly. Roll a few times in one direction, then go the other direction. Imagine that your head is a heavy ball and the weight of it is taking your neck around in a circle. Go slowly and breathe deeply. Figure 6-P

FIGURE 6-Q

BOW: Lie down on your stomach. Bend your legs, reach back and take hold of your ankles. Breathe in and stretch up like a bow. Breathe and relax, then begin rocking up and down like a rocking horse. Relax on your stomach for a few seconds after you do it for a minute. Figure 6-Q

FIGURE 6-R

HALF-BOW: Lie on your stomach. Clasp your hands behind your back with your fingers interlocked. Now breathe in and stretch your upper body up high, pulling your arms up straight. Leave your legs on the ground relaxed. Keep stretching for a time, breathing deeply. Then relax down. Figure 6-R

FIGURE 6-S

AIR WALK: Lie down on your back. Begin to walk in the air. Keep your right leg straight and lift it up as you lift the left arm. Breathe in as you lift, breathe out as your arm and leg go down. Then inhale again and lift the left leg and the right arm together. Exhale down. Keep going. Pretend you're walking on the ceiling. Figure 6-S

FIGURE 6-T

SWIMMING: Stand up. Bring your arms straight out to the sides. Begin to "swim" the arms backwards together in big circles. Both arms move back at the same time. Breathe strongly and go fast. Figure 6-T

FIGURE 6-U

THE BIG STRETCH: Stand up. Stretch up on your toes as you stretch your arms up over your head. Begin walking around on your toes. How tall can you be? Breathe...breathe...breathe! Figure 6-U

FIGURE 6-V

WINDMILLS: Stand with your feet comfortably apart. Bring your arms out to the sides. Breathe in. Now breathe out and bend and twist a little so that you can touch your right hand to the left foot. Your other arm will stretch straight up toward the sky. Look up at the arm pointed toward the sky. Breathe in and straighten up. Then breathe out and bend, touching the left hand to the right foot. Keep going for a minute. Figures 6-V and 6-W

FIGURE 6-W

FIGURE 6-X

"I AM" SWING: Stand up like you did for Windmills. Stretching your arms to the side, inhale and at the same time twist your body to the left, keeping your left arm straight. Touch your right hand to your heart and say "I AM" as you swing. Then, inhale and swing to the right side, touching your heart with your left hand, and again say "I AM." Feel that you are you. Repeat several times to each side. Figure 6-X

FIGURE 6-Y

VENUS STRETCH: Stand up. Interlock your fingers behind your back and stretch them up as you bend forward as far as you can. Stay relaxed and stretch more as you breathe in and out for a minute. Figure 6-Y

FIGURE 6-Z

TICKLE TABLE: Have you ever heard of a Tickle Table? Well, now is your chance to meet one and...it's YOU! Put your feet on the floor and your hands in back of you. Lift yourself up so that your body makes a flat table. Your head will be a little bit back. Since you are a human table, you are able to be tickled. And here come some invisible fingers, to tickle you until you can't stand it. Your table begins wriggling up and down, and your mouth begins laughing! Go to it and make a lot of noise as you wriggle and jiggle. Figure 6-Z

FIGURE 6-1

FIGURE 6-2

FIGURE 6-3

FIGURE 6-4

YOGA JACKS: These are jumping jacks, yoga style! Stand up with your feet together and your arms down at your sides. Breathe in and jump so that your feet are shoulder-width apart and your arms are out to the sides. Breathe out and jump again. This time your feet will be even further apart and your hands will clap over your head. Breathe in and come back to arms out, feet closer together. Then breathe out and return to the position you started in. To help you get started, try counting 1-2-3-4. Figures 6-1, 6-2, 6-3, and 6-4

FIGURE 6-5

LOTUS FLOWER: Sit with your feet together, like in Butterfly pose. Grab onto the bottoms of your feet from the inside where your big toe is. Your fingers will be on the bottoms of your feet and your thumbs will be on the top of your feet. Lean back. Hold onto your feet as you straighten your legs and stretch them up. They will spread apart. Straighten your back and concentrate on keeping your balance. You might want to focus your eyes on something in the distance to keep your balance. Breathe and stay up as long as you can. Can you time it and try to beat your own record? Figure 6-5

FIGURE 6-6

BUNDLE ROLL: Would you like to know what it feels like to be a log rolling down a hill? Try this: Lie down on your back with your legs straight and your arms down at your sides. Wiggle yourself back and forth until you flip over. Keep rolling from back to stomach, and back again, over and over. Remember—you are a log and a log does not bend! Figure 6-6

FIGURE 6-7

EARTHQUAKE: Stand with your feet close together. Interlace your fingers, and bring your arms straight up over your head. Keep an upward pull as the earthquake moves through you. It starts in your feet and legs. Begin to shake and shimmy them, keeping the feet in place on the floor. Then keep moving your legs but add your tail and stomach area. Shake your chest, shoulders, arms, and head. Everything should shake and shimmy in your own private earthquake! Figure 6-7

FIGURE 6-8

NOTE: Some of the following poses do not have corresponding pictures. They are repeated in a sitting, kneeling, and standing position.

TINY SEED: Imagine you are a tiny seed deep in the earth. Feel how dark and quiet it is where you are. Sit on your heels and put your forehead on the floor, arms at your side. Breathe. Figure 6-8

FIGURE 6-9

The tiny seed is beginning to feel something happen to it. It is beginning to grow. A tiny green plant is stretching up out of the ground. Begin to stretch your arms up over your head and sit up on your heels.

The wind blows the tiny plant. Bend side to side with your arms up and blow through your mouth. Figure 6-9

The rain beats down on the tiny plant. Bend forward and back up with your arms above your head. "Drip, drip, drip."

The sun shines down. Stretch back and feel the sun. Lean back as far as you can.

FIGURE 6-10

All these things help the little plant grow bigger. Grow bigger by straightening your body while kneeling up.

Here comes the wind again. Bend side to side sitting up on your knees.

And the rain... Bend forward and come back up a few times. Figure 6-10

And the sun shines. Stretch back and feel the sun!

And now our little plant is growing much bigger. Stand up, still with your arms up.

Here comes the wind to blow the plant. Do side bends and blow like the wind.

FIGURE 6-11

Here comes the rain to beat down on our plant. Bend forward and up, forward and up.

And now the sun comes. Feel the sun! Stretch back with arms up. Figure 6-11

And all these things help the little plant to grow into a great big...TREE! Now we are as tall as we can be! Stretch up on your toes. Think about what kind of big tree you are.

FIGURE 7-A

7. for two or more

ROW YOUR BOAT: Sit across from your friend with your legs out straight and opened wide. Decide which of you will have your legs on the bottom and which will have your legs on top of the other. Sit close enough together so you can hold hands. One of you goes forward while the other goes back. Now sing "Row, row, row your boat." Try to go all the way back and forward but remember it is a gentle stretch. Figure 7-A

FIGURE 7-B

CROW SQUATS: Stand up and face your partner holding both of her hands. Your feet are shoulder-width apart. Say "hello," and keep talking as you go down with your partner, and then up with your partner. Squat down, keeping your feet flat on the floor if you can, and your back straight. Find out more about your friend as you go up and down! Keep going for a minute, then thank each other at the end. Figure 7-B

FIGURE 7-C

YOGA TWISTS: Stand up facing your partner and hold onto one another on the upper arms. Now greet each other and begin Yoga Twists, twisting side-to-side, in opposite directions from each other, like a turbo washing machine. Go for it for a minute or two. Figure 7-C

FIGURE 7-D

DOUBLE LOTUS FLOWER: Sit across from each other. Scoot up close enough so that you can make a "foot sandwich" with each of your partner's feet. Hold hands in the middle. Breathe in, lean back a little, and stretch both your legs up in the air at the same time as your partner. Keep your feet together with your partner's. Pretend they are glued together. Look at each other and smile! Keep breathing! Figure 7-D

FIGURE 7-E

WASHING WINDOWS: Sit across from your partner with your legs crossed. Sit very straight, look into each other's eyes, and offer a greeting. Put the palms of your hands together with your partner's. Pretend you are washing a window. Move your hands slowly in circles with your partner. Try to tune into your partner, and she will tune in with you. Try to move where she wants to move, and she will move where you want to move. Be sensitive and keep going for a minute. Figure 7-E

THE SUNFLOWER: This works best if there are four or more of you. Sit down in a circle with everyone's legs stretched out in the center. These are the petals of the sunflower. Close the petals by stretching forward and touching your toes, bringing your face close to your knees (Figure 7-F). Begin the story when everyone is ready:

"It is night and the sunflower is sleeping with its petals closed....Now something is beginning to happen. The morning is dawning and the sunflower begins to open." Start to sit up slowly and open your arms as you breathe in. Figure 7-G

"As the sun gets hotter and the day goes on, the sunflower opens all the way." Slowly keep leaning back, controlling the movement with your stomach muscles, until you are lying on the floor with your arms out to the sides. Breathe out as you go down.

"The sunflower stays open all day, enjoying the warm sun on its face." Relax and stay open.

"Now the sun is beginning to go down." Using your stomach muscles to help you, sit up very slowly. Let your arms be out in front to help you pull up slowly. Breathe in.

"The sun is going down completely now, and it is getting dark. The sunflower closes up and rests for the night." Slowly lean forward and rest your hands on your legs or toes. Breathe out gently. Figure 7-F again

You can tell the sunflower's story again, if you like.

FIGURE 7-F

FIGURE 7-G

FIGURE 8-A

8. to be is to breathe

One thing that everyone does is breathe. You don't even have to think about it—it just happens! But have you ever taken a deep breath on purpose, say, to smell a beautiful rose? That is called being aware of your breath. When you do it often, you feel happier and more relaxed. Here are some breathing games for you to try.

BALLOONS: Sit with your legs crossed and your back straight. Bring your hands together at your chest. Did you know that your lungs are like balloons inside of you? As you breathe in, you fill up these balloons with fresh air and energy. As you breathe out, you empty the balloons of old air and energy. Try imagining this as you stretch your arms up on the inhale. Then blow out as you bring your arms down to your chest.

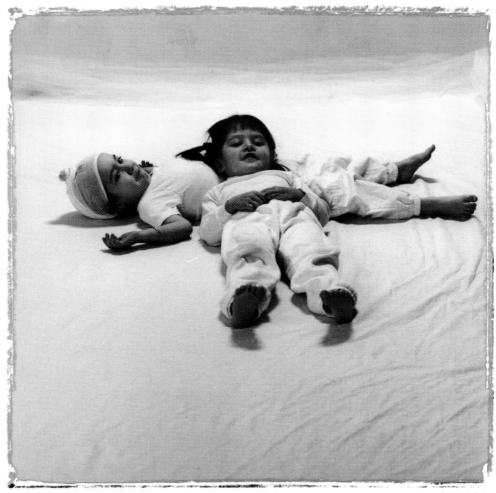

FIGURE 8-B

BIRTHDAY CANDLES: Sit with your legs crossed and your back straight. Breathe in deeply. Imagine seeing your birthday cake with all its bright candles, and blow them out, breathing out strongly through your mouth. As you inhale through your nose, stretch your arms up and out. As you blow out strongly through your mouth, bring them back together at the center of your chest. Figure 8-A (on page 86)

PILLOWS: Lie down on your back. Have your friend lie down on her back so your stomach is her pillow. Take a deep breath and fill up your belly with the breath. Did your friend feel her head move? Now breathe out from your belly. Make it flatten. Is her pillow moving again? Try it a few more times. Now switch places with your friend and feel your pillow move! Call all your friends and make a whole line of moving pillows! Figure 8-B

"REALLY COOL" BREATH: This cools you out when you're super upset, really mad, and ready to punch someone! It also works when you are really excited and need to calm yourself down. What you are going to do is make your tongue into a kind of "straw" by opening your mouth and pulling up the sides of your tongue in a "U" shape. Now take a deep breath in through your curled tongue, close your mouth, and breathe out through your nose. Notice how cool your breath feels as it goes in? That means it's working! You might like to look in a mirror to get it right. After you've had a good laugh at how funny it looks, try it for a few minutes with your eyes closed and...be cool! Figure 8-C

P.S. Some of us can't curl our tongue. It is just not the way we are made. If you have been trying and your tongue is just not co-operating with you, don't give up! You can still "be cool." Just open your mouth, put out your tongue a little, and breathe in slowly. Sip the air. It will feel cool, and it will work for you!

YOU ARE GREAT: Try putting an affirmation on your breath. "Affirmation" is a big word for saying something good to yourself. Like, try "I Am Happy." Think of it as you breathe in. Then breathe out and think, "I Am Good." Here's another one: "I Am Brave, I Am Bold, My Own Spirit I Can Hold." (Hmm, sounds like it could be a great song too. Singing is an excellent way to use your breath!) Figure 8-D

FIGURE 8-D

89

FIGURE 9-A

9. deep relaxation time

Now it's time to lie down on your back, with your legs and arms down by your sides, and the palms of your hands facing up and relaxed. To stay cozy, cover yourself with a light blanket. Breathe gently through your nose. Choose one of these relaxation stories and have someone read it to you VERY slowly. Figure 9-A

DEEP RELAXATION: Close your eyes, and begin to relax your whole body. Start with your feet, then move up and relax your legs. Send your breath into your feet and legs to relax them. Now relax your back, stomach, and chest. Relax, relax, relax... Send a relaxing feeling into your arms and hands. Feel the warm feeling go down your arms. Use your breath and imagination to help you. Now breathe and relax your shoulders, neck, and head. Relax your face. As you breathe, feel yourself sinking down, down, into the center of you. As your body rests peacefully on the ground, feel a light all around you. Keep relaxing quietly or have someone slowly and softly count to 25 while you relax. See if you can be perfectly still, and perfectly relaxed.

THE BEACH STORY: Imagine you are lying on the beach. The warm sand feels so comfortable on your back. Feel the sun warming up your whole body. As you breathe in, listen! It sounds like the waves coming up to the shore. As you breathe out, imagine the waves going back out to sea. Keep breathing with the waves for another moment or two. In your open hands, imagine you have some birdseed for the seagulls. Imagine the seagulls circling around you. They want to come down and take the birdseed, but they feel a little afraid. Make yourself very peaceful and quiet so they will know you are a friend. Breathe and relax for a minute, allowing the seagulls to come.

CLOUD: Imagine a very soft, white cloud has come down to take you for a ride. Feel yourself going up, up, up into the beautiful blue sky. The gentle wind is in your face. It almost feels like you are riding on air, but you can see puffs of white clouds all around you, like angels. Breathe gently as you travel through the sky. Look around for a minute... Ahead of you is a rainbow. You can see that your cloud is going to travel right through the rainbow. As you pass through each color, feel that color wash over you, and feel the happiness it brings. Red...then orange...yellow...green..then blue...and purple. And once again you are traveling through the sky. Now your cloud is lowering you gently down, down, down. One...two...three...four...five... and you are down on the ground again. Inside yourself say a "thank you" to the cloud for the special ride.

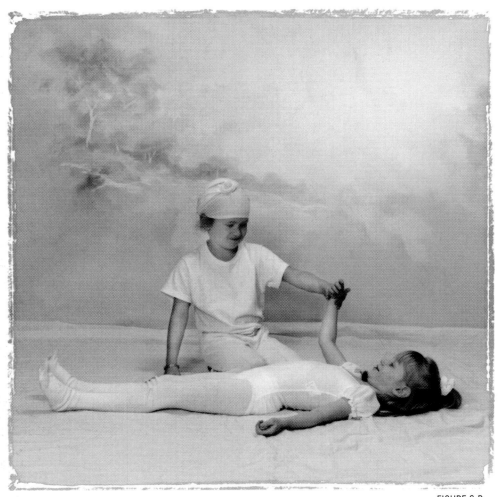

FIGURE 9-B

THE SPAGHETTI TEST: After you get yourself all relaxed, have a friend or parent give you the "spaghetti test." Have you ever seen spaghetti when it is uncooked? It is very stiff. But what happens to it when it's been cooked? That's right—it becomes all floppy. When you pick it up it will move in whatever direction you make it move. That is what you want your arms and legs to be able to do. Imagine that you are cooked spaghetti. Then have a friend or parent "test" you to see if you are "done." The other person will pick up your arm or leg VERY GENTLY. Figure 9-B

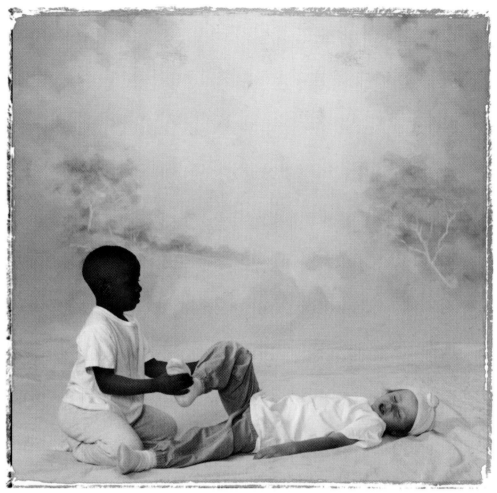

FIGURE 9-C

Then they will gently move your arm or leg to see if it is floppy. Keep yourself relaxed. Don't help them lift, but don't pull back either. Pretend you are asleep, and just ALLOW them to move your floppy arm or leg. When they are done testing you, they will gently lay your arm or leg back down. Figure 9-C

FIGURE 10-A

10. wake-up exercises

Which do you think feels better to your body after it has been resting—to open your eyes and jump up or to wake up little by little? Did you guess that the best thing you can do is to wake yourself up little by little? If you did, you are right! Here are some exercises to wake up your body in a smooth and gentle way:

TINY CIRCLES: Breathe in deeply, breathe out deeply. Then roll your wrists and ankles in little circles. Do this for 20 seconds. Figure 10-A

FIGURE 10-B

CRICKET RUB: Pick up your feet and begin to rub the bottoms of your feet together. Rub your hands together at the same time. Do this for 20 seconds. Figure 10-B

HEALING HANDS: Put your feet down, but keep rubbing your hands. When they feel very warm, put your hands over your face, covering your eyes. Send healing energy and warmth into your eyes. Breathe deeply. Figure 10-C

FIGURE 10-D

CAT STRETCH: Lie down on your back. Put your arms out to the sides on the ground. Bend one knee and stretch that leg across your body to the floor on the other side of you. Stretch the way a cat stretches after she has been sleeping. Then do the same with the other leg. Figure 10-D

FIGURE 10-E

ROCK AND ROLL: Tuck yourself up into a tiny ball by wrapping your arms around your knees and placing your nose between your knees. Rock back and forth on your spine. Rock all the way 'til you're sitting up and all the way back onto your shoulders. Roll side to side too. Do this several times. Figure 10-E

FIGURE 11-A

11. five meditations for happiness

What is meditation? It is quieting yourself enough to hear the universe speak to you. It is letting go of unhappy, angry, or scary thoughts and feelings, and knowing you are bigger than they are. It is feeling the love that you are, the peace that you are, and the hero that you are. And you know what? After you've begun to meditate regularly, you will have your own things to say about what meditation is, and they will be different from what I've said. And they will be just as true!

GET READY: Sit with your legs crossed, or try Lotus Pose. This is done by bringing each foot up to where the legs and body meet. Your body will look like a pretzel! This creates a lock that automatically makes your spine totally straight. Figure 11-A

FIGURE 11-B

If you prefer to sit in a cross-legged position, this will work fine too. Just remember to keep your spine straight. Why is that so important? Well, let's think of a
garden hose for a minute. What happens to it when it is bent? Can the water flow
through it? When it is straightened, what happens to the water? Does it flow
more freely? Your spine is your hose. Energy flows through the spine. When you
meditate do you want your energy to flow with strength? Then you will want to
make your back straight and tall, chest up and out, neck straight, chin slightly
tucked in. Think of a puppet on a string and how its body straightens when the
string is tugged from above by the puppeteer. Try it on yourself. Figure 11-B

It is good to keep the spine warm when you meditate, so you may want to have a light covering for your back as you sit. Then choose one of these five meditations.

SILENT MEDITATION:

Sit straight and tall. Place your hands on your knees with your palms up. Place your fingers in "wise pose," which means that your first finger and your thumb are touching, and the other fingers are out straight. Your hands will rest on your knees.

Be as tall and steady as a mountain. It has been around for millions of years. Be a pyramid. Be built to last thousands of years. Be straight, steady, and silently wise. Don't move no matter what. Your mind will tell you that you have to move, but don't listen to it! Breathe instead—a long, light breath. Don't move a muscle, but be perfectly relaxed as you sit in perfectly silent, still meditation for one minute. When you can do it perfectly, add one minute. Each day add another until you've reached your goal of 5 or 10 minutes. If you really get inspired, go for a half-hour! Figure 11-B again

"I AM, I AM" MEDITATION:
Sit with a straight spine. Your
right hand will be down on
your leg in "Wise Pose," your
left hand will be at your heart
level. Make your palm flat
with the fingers straight and
pointing to the right. Look at
your hand the whole time,
but with your eyes mostly
closed. Start with your hand
six inches away from you,
then move it a few inches
closer to your chest as you
say the first "I AM." Then
move your hand so that it is
one foot away from you and
say "I AM" again. Keep
repeating the sequence. Do it
slowly and put yourself into
it. The close-up "I AM" means
"I AM who I know myself to
be." The far away "I AM"
means "I AM that which is
greater than I know myself to
be." Start with a few minutes
each day and add to it as you
go. Figures 11-C and 11-D

FIGURE 11-C

FIGURE 11-D

FIGURE 11-E

NO/YES MEDITATION: Sit like a pyramid, with hands in "Wise Pose." Close your eyes. Think of all the times you wanted to say "no," and say it now. Say it fast, slow, soft, loud—however you feel like it. Go on for a minute or two. Then inhale, exhale and do the same for "yes." Get out all your "NOs," then all your "YESes," and feel GOOD!

Really let yourself feel each no and yes. Get into it and go! At the end, say one or two minutes of SA TA NA MA to balance yourself. (See next page for instructions.) Add more time to your meditation as your practice goes on. Figures 11-E and 11-F

FIGURE 11-F

SA TA NA MA MEDITATION:

This meditation is called the "Garbage Truck" because it cleans out all the "garbage" from your mind, even the yucky stuff that is stuck way down in the bottom! Your angry feelings about something that happened at school, your hurt feelings about something that happened at home...it hauls all the trash away!

Have you ever taken a Karate or Kung Fu class? You know how there are certain sounds that you make that help you focus and add energy to your kicks? Well, there are "yoga sounds" too. SA TA NA MA are some of those sounds. They give you focus and add a certain kind of energy to your meditation. Here's how to use them:

Say "SAAH" and press your thumb and first finger together.

On "TAAH" press your thumb and middle finger together.

On "NAAH" press your thumb and ring finger together.

And on "MAAH" press your thumb and little finger together.

Now that you're a master at SA TA NA MA, you are ready to graduate into "Black Belt" meditation. Here's how:

1. Say it out loud for about 1 minute.

2. Whisper it for the same amount of time.

3. Hear it inside yourself while you silently keep moving your fingers for one minute.

4. Do another minute of silence, then one minute of whispering, then one minute of saying it out loud.

That will add up to how much? Right—six minutes!

If you are new at this, you could start with 30 seconds for each section, which would add up to 3 minutes. You can keep adding a minute to each section as you continue with your meditation practice. But don't go any longer than 5 minutes for each, which would add up to....you guessed it—30 minutes. If you can do that, jump up and shake yourself for a minute. Then congratulate yourself for graduating into "Black Belt" meditation!

FIGURE 11-G

MEDITATION TO TAKE AWAY THOUGHTS YOU DON'T LIKE:
This is my son, Ram Das Singh. He is 6 years old in this photograph. He uses this meditation when he has a thought or a feeling that he doesn't like, and it keeps coming up over and over. Here is what he has to say about this meditation:

"You inhale and think of the thought you don't want. Then you exhale by blowing into your hands and that bad thought or feeling will be destroyed by going down into your hands, which are like a pool of water, and the water sucks it in. This is the way I imagine it. You might imagine something else." Figure 11-G

FIGURE 11-H

Now, sit with a straight spine. Make a cup with your hands by putting your right hand inside the left. Your fingers will cross each other. Put this open cup in front of you at the heart level. Your eyes will look only into this cup. Breathe in deeply through the nose. Breathe out through the mouth in a long, slow, blowing motion, almost like a dry spitting motion. Blow the thought into the cup. Continue like this for a few minutes, adding more time as you keep practicing. At the end of your meditation, close your eyes and feel your spine. Starting at the top, feel it all the way down to the bottom. Feel it as if you are feeling a stick in your hand. The more you can feel the whole spine all the way to the bottom, the more your meditation will be able to help you. Then inhale...exhale and relax. Figure 11-H

❋ ❋ ❋ ❋ ❋ THE REAL COOKIE ❋ ❋ ❋ ❋ ❋

Many years ago in a faraway land lived a boy named Farid (Fa REED). Everyone agreed that he was a very special boy, very bright, very kind, and with a wisdom beyond his years. His mother, being very wise herself, decided on a plan to help Farid have the experience of meditation.

She set up a little mat in the backyard under a large tree. Under the mat she put a cookie. Then she went to Farid and said, "My dear son. Our Creator is very sweet, and gives sweets to those who meditate." Farid smiled at his mother mischievously and answered, "In how much time, mother?" To which she replied, "In about one-half hour." So laughing, he sat down, straightened his spine, closed his eyes, and began meditating within himself on the Creator of all.

This went on for a while, perhaps a month or more, every day the same. Farid would sit on his mat under the big tree. He would meditate for half an hour. Then he would open his eyes, lift up the mat, and find the sweet cookie waiting for him there.

One day, Farid's mother was making dinner in her kitchen when she realized Farid had been meditating for more than his usual one-half hour. She looked out of the window to see him sitting quite still under the tree. Deciding that he must have forgotten about the time, she ran over to him, calling, "Farid! Farid! Your meditation time is over." But he did not move. She touched him softly, so as not to disturb his meditation rudely, but he still did not move. He sat totally still, with a very slight smile upon his face. If his mother had not been so concerned for him, she might have noticed a soft and peaceful glow surrounding him. Instead she began to shake him, and speaking much more loudly, saying, "Wake up! Wake up, Farid!"

At this, Farid slowly opened his eyes, and his smile grew wider. He seemed to have grown as wise as a sage, and to have as much love in his heart as a saint, in just that short time of meditation. His mother was feeling very confused about what had happened. "Farid, are you all right? Here, have your cookie. Have you forgotten to eat it?"

With love shining from his eyes, Farid replied, "You may have this cookie if you like, mother. Today I got the REAL cookie. And mother, it was so sweet!"

(Farid was a real person. He grew up to be a well-know Sufi saint. Perhaps you would like to try having a cookie under your mat when you meditate?)

12. the "long time sun" song

To end your yoga class, there is a beautiful song you can sing to wish each other well, to send a good thought to someone you love, and to celebrate yourself. Sit up straight and sing from your heart. There are special arm movements that you can do as you sing this good-bye song.

FIGURE 12-A

FIGURE 12-B

May the long time sun shine upon you, (Sweep your arms upward, making a circle above your head. Figure 12-A)

All love surround you, (Bring your arms down towards your body and then stretch your arms in front of you in a sweeping motion. Figure 12-B)

FIGURE 12-C

FIGURE 12-D

And the pure light within you
(Cross your arms over your heart.
Figure 12-C)

Guide your way on, Guide your way on.
(Move your arms away from your chest
and circle your hands around each other.
Figure 12-D)

And the pure light with - in you, guide your way on, guide your way on.

13. how does it help me?

The names of the exercises in this book are listed here in alphabetical order. Look for the name you want. Then read about how that yoga exercise helps you. Note that special yoga names are listed in parentheses.

AIR WALK: Helps to coordinate both sides of the brain. May help with learning disabilities.

ARCHER: Brings courage and focus.

BABY POSE: Relaxes your entire body and helps you feel peaceful.

BALANCE POSE: Strengthens your abdomen. Helps to coordinate your mind and body.

BEAR WALK: Brings balance to your emotions.

BEAUTIFUL BIRD: Loosens your upper spine.

BICYCLE: Helps digestion, and massages lymph glands.

BIG STRETCH: Good for your glands. Stretches your spine.

BOULDER: Massages your spine, helps digestion.

BOW POSE: Good for circulation and digestion.

BUBBLE POP: Relaxes pelvis, strengthens lower back and sciatic nerve.

BUMPY CAMEL: Gives you a flexible spine, allowing energy to flow throughout your body. (SPINE FLEX)

BUNDLE ROLL: Stimulates and relaxes your entire body.

BUTTERFLY: Brings flexibility to your hips and pelvis.

BUTTERFLY/COCOON: Strengthens your abdominal area and helps you feel radiant.

BUZZING BEE: Massages your elbows, releases tension from your shoulders.

CANDLE: Allows energy to flow to your upper spine and releases tension. (SHOULDER STAND)

CANDLE SPLIT: Good for your upper spine and sciatic nerve.

CAT AND COW: Helps bring flexibility to your spine and energizes you.

CAT STRETCH: Relaxes your back.

COBRA: Helps to release tension from your muscles.

CRAB WALK: Good for your spine, glands, and coordination.

CRICKET RUB: Good for circulation to your hands and feet. Helps to break up calcium deposits.

CROW SQUAT: Relaxes your pelvis and lower spine.

DEEP RELAXATION: Allows your body to integrate the yoga that you just finished.

DINOSAUR WALK: Helps you to move food through your body. Prepares you to meditate.

DONKEY KICK: Energizes your brain.

DOUBLE LOTUS FLOWER: Gives you balance and radiance.

DRYER: Energizes you and helps to bring your mind into focus.

EARTHQUAKE: Helps to balance the minerals in your body. Helps support and maintain a healthy immune system.

EASY "V": Strengthens your abdominal muscles.

ELEPHANT: Keeps your spine flexible. Good for your circulation.

FISH POSE: Helps to balance the minerals in your body.

FROG POSE: Helps to circulate energy to the upper body. Good for your eyes, heart, and glands.

HALF-BOW: Good for your lymph glands.

HEALING HANDS: Relaxes your eyes.

"I AM" SWING: Good for your heart and intestines.

JOGGING: Helps your heart and circulation.

KANGAROO HOPS: Helps to put you in control of your body and mind.

LION POSE: Brings energy to your shoulders and throat.

LOTUS FLOWER: Brings energy to your heart and brain. (KUNDALINI LOTUS)

LOTUS POSE: Straightens your spine for meditation.

MONKEY JUMP: Helps to keep your glands working well.

MOUNTAIN POSE: Good for digestion and your nervous system. Helps release anger. (TRIANGLE POSE)

NECK ROLL: Relaxes your neck, brings energy to the brain.

NO HANDS STAND: Balances inflow and outflow of energy in your body.

PENGUIN: Helps with coordination and improves circulation.

PLOW: Good for energizing you and relaxing your back muscles.

RAIN CLOUD: Helps keep away illness and disease. (CAMEL)

ROCK 'N' ROLL: Helps to digest food and massages your spine.

ROW YOUR BOAT: Strengthens your abdominal area. Helps to calm your mind.

SEAL: Helps to strengthen your nerves and your digestive and abdominal muscles. (EXTENDED LOCUST)

SHOULDER SHRUGS: Releases tension from your shoulders. Helps bring energy to the brain.

SLIDING BOARD: Strengthens your lower spine and arms. (BACK PLATFORM)

SPIDER STRETCH: Good for your glandular system. (CHAIR POSE)

SUNFLOWER: Helps to balance your glands. Strengthens your abdomen and calms your mind.

SWIMMING: Good for your heart.

TALL GRASS: Good for brain coordination and your immune system.

THUNDER AND LIGHTNING: Stretches your spine and keeps it flexible. Cannon breath energizes you.

TICKLE TABLE: Helps your glands. Laughing releases tension.

TINY CIRCLES: Releases tension in your hands and feet and wakes them up.

TINY SEED: Good for your rib cage, entire spine, and circulation.

TRAIN RIDE: Loosens up your spine. Good for digestion. (SPINE FLEX)

TRAIN WHEELS: Good for your rib cage and digestion.

TREE POSE: Helps to keep spine in alignment.

UP THE HILL: Stretches your legs out. Relaxes your upper and lower spine.

VENUS STRETCH: Stretches and relaxes your shoulders and energizes your brain.

WALKING IN PLOW: Helps to support emotional balance.

WASHING MACHINE: Releases tension from your upper spine.

WASHING WINDOWS: Sensitizes you to other people.

WHEEL POSE: Relaxes your lower back. Allows energy to flow through the entire spine.

WINDMILLS: Good for your nervous system.

WINDSTORM: Helps your liver, colon, and stomach.

WOODCHOPPER: Relaxes your ribcage. Energizes you.

YOGA JACKS: Makes your mind clear and helps to balance your entire body.

YOGA TWISTS: Good for your liver.

appendix

As you may know, yoga is an ancient science from the East. It is not a religion, or affiliated with any religion, and it can be practiced and experienced by all regardless of religious preference. The word "yoga" means to yoke, or unite. Yoga unites the physical, mental, and spiritual aspects of a person.

The kind of yoga you find in this book is called Kundalini yoga. As taught by Yogi Bhajan, it is a form of physical exercise that, with practice, awakens the creative energy or "Kundal" within you. This dormant energy can be equated with the human potential, and when it is activated, life just gets better and better!

resources

For more information about Kundalini Yoga classes in your area, or to find out about healthful living resources, contact the 3HO Foundation (Healthy, Happy, Holy Organization):

phone: 505-753-0423 (in U.S.A.)

fax: 505-753-5982

e-mail: kyta@newmexico.com

homepage: www.3ho.org

RESOURCE CATALOG:

Ancient Healing Ways: Tools for Body, Mind, and Spirit

1-800-359-2940 (in U.S.A.)

505-747-2860 (outside of U.S.A.)

about the author

Shakta Kaur Khalsa has been practicing and teaching Kundalini Yoga since 1976. Her teacher is Yogi Bhajan, Ph.D., master of Kundalini Yoga and head of the Sikh faith in the Western Hemisphere.

Shakta lives in Herndon, Virginia, just outside of Washington, D.C., with her husband and their son. She has been a Montessori teacher since 1981, and a former owner-director of a school. She has worked with children in many capacities, from directing and teaching at summer camps internationally to teaching yoga and music to pre-schoolers and elementary-age children in her area. All of the children in this book have been her students.

After 20 years of teaching yoga and children and loving them both, the union of the two became obvious. This book is the perfectly natural result of that union.